BIRACIAL BLUES

Charleston, SC
www.PalmettoPublishing.com

Biracial Blues
Copyright © 2023 by Ariel Amanda

Hardcover ISBN: 979-8-8229-1336-3
Paperback ISBN: 979-8-8229-1337-0
eBook ISBN: 979-8-8229-1338-7

BIRACIAL
BLUES
Being Biracial in a
black & white world
Ariel Amanda

DEDICATION

To Christina Harris, Kaiden Pabon, Joshua Richardson, Kaysin
Ramsey:
I hope you never feel like you don't belong.

INTELLIGENCE IS NOT ATTRIBUTED TO COLOR

~ JAY-Z

INTRODUCTION

For a long time, I didn't know what it meant to be "half and half." Although I didn't know what it meant, I attempted to explain the meaning of being biracial as a child. Looking at the after-school program teacher, I confidently said, "Half Black means that this side of me is black," gesturing with my hands to one side of my face, "and this side is White." To me, being biracial was physical. I'd known I was half Black as far back as I could remember, but what's sad is I didn't know what ethnicity or race was. Who told me or how I was told I don't remember, but there was never a time that I didn't know I was biracial. I also didn't know who my biological father was until my preteen years. I just knew he was Black, and his name was Gregory.

I know you might be wondering why I'm telling you this. For a long time, I struggled with identity and who I was, mainly because people around me led me to believe that my ethnicity defined who I was as a person. See, that's the way America works. When someone first meets you, unless you have what they consider clear-cut features of your ethnicity, they ask, "What are you? What race are you?" And just by learning that information, they think they know you.

To be clear, I didn't struggle with identity because I was half Black; I struggled because I didn't look like my family, and I wasn't raised by my dad, to whom I looked more similar. My mom's side of the family is Puerto Rican, and according to others, I didn't have Puerto Rican features. Because I didn't know what it meant to be "half and half," I grew depressed for a while. I'd tell people I was Puerto Rican and Black, and they'd twist up their faces in confusion, disgust, or disbelief.

I was born in the early '90s. Where I was from, being biracial was uncommon. I battled isolation, stereotypes, and racism. Yes—all in the late '90s and early 2000s. I didn't let it defeat me; I let it build me. But I had to journey through many stages of my life to get to that point. In this book, I'll tell my story in five steps that I consider like the five stages of grief. I want to teach you how to kill insecurity the same way I did. By the end of this book, you'll love who you are regardless of your race, ethnicity, or nationality!

STAGE ONE: DENIAL

"The Jim Crow laws were created to enforce segregation," my teacher passionately spoke as he taught my third grade class about a time in history where segregation was legal. He was a tall white man with blue eyes and sandy brown hair, and everyone feared him because of his strict classroom rules. The year before, when I was in second grade, my classmates and I talked about how none of us wanted to be in his class. Rumor was he hit kids with rulers and yelled all the time.

"What segregation means?" Anthony Lee asked.

"Segregation means separation. It was a time in history where it was legal to separate people based on the color of their skin, by their race," the teacher replied.

The class was silent. It seemed as if everyone was deep in thought or was trying to make sense of it. I was one of the people trying to put the pieces together because it just didn't make sense to me.

For the rest of the period, we talked about slavery, Dr. Martin Luther King, Jr., and others like him. It was when we discussed Rosa Parks that she said it to me, her face scrunched up with a look of pure disgust.

"*I hate white people!*" Tyra said, looking me in my eyes without blinking.

My face turned red, my heart sank, and if I were any lower in my seat, I would've been curled under my desk. On top of being embarrassed, I was extremely confused about why she was calling me white when my mom always said I was Puerto Rican and Black. I fought back the tears as my whole class—where I was the only "different" one—stared at me, scowling as if I were Jim Crow himself. My teacher said nothing, turned back to the board, and began writing the next assignment.

As much as I hated him for not protecting me, there was nothing he could do. He was a white man, tall, with sand-colored hair and eyes as blue as the ocean. Sometimes when I thought back on that moment, I wondered if he hadn't said anything because he didn't know my ethnicity, or maybe it was because he was uncomfortable teaching Black history in an urban community school. Either way, he didn't step in to stop what was happening.

I spent lunch alone that day because my entire class scooted to the other side of the bench as if I were contagious. I barely touched my lunch. Confusing thoughts filled my brain and made my head spin. Was I really white, and were my ancestors responsible for this? I couldn't grasp the thought. It felt like warm vomit sat at the back of my throat.

Out on the playground, I sat on the swing set, replaying the words she spouted at me, *"I hate white people. I hate white people."*

"Ariel!" I heard my name called from far away and tried to look in the same direction. I stood up, still not seeing anyone, but I was desperate to have a friend at that moment. I felt a push on my right shoulder, and when I turned around, the pain from someone's hand stung me on my right cheek. I held my cheek, feeling a mixture of shame and frustration. I finally realized it was Tyra when she said, "White bitch," along with three other girls I didn't know. Together they took turns pushing me back and forth until I finally fell down. I crouched in the fetal position to hide my face. I didn't want anyone to see that I was crying. The tears streamed down my face, not because I was in pain physically but because I was hurting emotionally. I was angry about how different I was. My mom said I was half Black, but why didn't I look like it? I thought looking half-Black would have saved me from being in that situation. If I looked Black, I wouldn't be in the fetal position crying like a two-year-old.

That night I stared into space. Although I was home, feeling safe was out of the question. The next day would just be a replay of the day before. I felt so isolated, humiliated and agitated because nothing I could do would change what was wrong. To add to my frustration, I had no one whom I felt could understand me. No one looked like me.

One thing was for sure: I didn't want to go to school and face Tyra again. There was only one problem with that—Tyra lived in my neighborhood. What if she told everyone I was white? I lived in a neighborhood dominated by Hispanics and Blacks, but no one else around identified with me—bushy hair, thick eyebrows, dark freckles, full lips, light brown eyes with dark circles underneath, and fair, warm-ivory skin tone. It was a sharp contrast to the other girls whose features consisted of smooth brown skin, permed pigtails and braids. Or their skin was a fair tone, and they had light eyes, long, defined curls, or straight hair. See, their problem with me was that I had both features, and they could never pinpoint what race or ethnicity I was.

Tyra would sometimes come down from two buildings over to my stoop and attempt conversation. I didn't understand how she was friendly at home, but then she was the devil at school. One day I was coming across the street from the store when I heard someone yelling, "White girl; white girl!" Of course, it was Tyra, with her cousin Jade who came over most weekends. Jade was nine years old like us but looked like she was thirteen. She was known for picking on kids smaller than herself. When I looked up toward her window, she rolled her eyes, and her cousin stuck up her middle finger. Walking home, feelings of defeat crept up my spine.

I hoped for relief when my aunt Laura, my mom's eldest sister, braided my hair sometimes. I liked the idea of not combing my hair every day. Even more, When she first braided my hair, I believed that I'd fit in more because all the girls at school wore braids. My aunt even told me there was no need to put rubber bands at the ends of the braids to hold my hair in place. Excitement filled my heart at the thought of finally being accepted by the other girls and showing them that I was more like them than they thought.

At school, my newfound confidence motivated me to be more social. It didn't last long before Tyra and her gang of friends saw me and pointed and laughed at me in the hallway. When we got to class, Tyra stared at me hard before saying, "You trying to be Black!"

I yelled back at her, saying, "I am Black!"

The whole class laughed, and Tyra said, "NO! you *want* to be Black!"

I didn't have a comeback because she probably was right. So there I was, trying to fit in and look more like the other girls, but the situation had gotten worse. They all knew I was trying to blend in, which only made me stick out more. The crazy part was that I shouldn't have needed to blend in because I was in. My father was Black; it was painful that no one believed me though.

Incidents like this with Tyra continued for the next two years. From the second grade until the end of fourth grade, I did anything to avoid Tyra and her group of friends. After that, it just became a routine. Although the physical abuse seemed to calm down at some point, I never could see myself being friends with Tyra. She would always be the girl who labeled me. It was because of her that I began struggling with my identity. I hated her for that. But if I'm being honest with myself, I needed to face the fact that she wouldn't be the only person to isolate me.

In third grade, my Spanish teacher, Ms. R, asked me to read a Spanish sentence out loud. Although I felt a little confident while reading, afterward, she rolled her eyes and said words I will never forget: *"So much for a native speaker!"* She sounded as if she were both disappointed and exhausted. The class burst into laughter. After that day, I never attempted speaking Spanish again!

Finally, in September of 2002, I was changing schools because my family and I were moving to Georgia. Happiness glowed in me. Finally, there was a reason to feel excited because I'd be moving away from Tyra and the other girls at school, and I'd be starting fresh and meeting new people, maybe even making friends.

I was already familiar with Georgia because we took a family trip there every year to see my aunt Rachel, my mom's second eldest sister, uncle Fred, and their three girls. I loved going to Georgia to see them because we always had the best time together. We'd go to great restaurants, Disney World, which was not too far away in Florida, and other amusement parks. So I was excited to move close to them.

We moved to Waynesville, Georgia, when I was ten years old. Although we didn't live there for long, it was an experience I'll never forget. Our first week there, my mom and I attended the open house at the school I would be attending. My aunt and cousins had already lived in Georgia for a while, so they knew everybody. But I was a little nervous because I didn't know anyone there. Not only was I in a new school, but also I was far away from my hometown of North

New Jersey. Although I was nervous, it didn't matter much because I was still excited about being in a new school.

The school building was made of red brick and didn't look like any school I had seen back home. I was used to tall buildings with several floors, but this school was long, looked as if it occupied half of a block, and was only one floor. I was curious as to how many students could fit into a building with just one floor.

Walking into the school, I didn't hear a lot of the commotion I was used to hearing. Instead, faint whispers were coming from different directions like it was a library. The parents met the teachers in their classrooms while a lady, who I assumed was the principal, walked in and out of each classroom, introducing herself. Back-to-School Night at home was usually full of loud laughter, kids running around, and the noise of different conversations happening at once. It was so crowded that you had to squeeze your way into the main area and hope to find a seat. We used to leave an hour early just so we could find a seat and not have to stand for two hours. There we'd talk for a while to the families we knew in a big cafeteria until the principal got in the front and started rambling to the parents on a loud microphone. Even then, conversations continued until they grew too loud for anyone to hear the principal. Then, usually, someone started yelling, "SHUT UP!" One year a lady got punched in the nose after a heated argument broke out over a group of parents who wouldn't stop talking over the principal. But this new school wasn't crowded or noisy like that.

The classroom we sat in was small. It included fifteen desks crunched together, a whiteboard, and a small teacher's desk that sat in the corner away from the whiteboard. We took our seats at the far right of the room, where my aunt spoke with a lady named Nora. My aunt introduced Nora to my mom and me, then Nora introduced

Jena, her daughter. She said we could get to know one another since we'd be in the same class. Jena wore a pretty polka-dot dress with a fancy bow to match. Her smile was wide and welcoming. She looked pretty but dressed differently from how I was used to seeing girls dress. I wore dark blue jeans and a pink Baby Phat shirt with white Adidas sneakers, my hair in a low-braided ponytail. I was relieved to meet someone so nice because it calmed my nerves about the first day of school, especially since my cousin, who was the same age as I was, was assigned to a different class and wouldn't be able to keep me company. Jena and I talked for a little and assured one another we'd see each other on the first day of school.

On the first day of school, I scrambled to find clothes. I assumed everyone would be dressed like Jena, and I didn't want to give anyone a reason to pick on me. I asked my mom if I could wear my hair out since most of the girls there did. She said, "Heck no! Your hair is not the type of hair you can just leave out." She brushed it back in a braided ponytail, and I pouted the whole time. I settled for a pink short-sleeved shirt, dark blue capris and white sneakers. I looked in the mirror, not accepting my look, but I had to suck it up.

My emotions were all over the place the whole ride to school. Anxious but excited at the same time, the thought of being at a different school with new people made my stomach do flips. Before walking in, I paused to inhale a deep breath and prepared for what-ever would happen. Walking through the hallway with my head held high, I avoided any eye contact with anyone. I squeezed my eyes shut at the classroom door then opened it quickly to prevent any more anxiety. My pretend grin quickly faded away when everyone's dead silence at the sight of me took over every emotion in my body.

I saw Jena in the corner of the class with two other girls, but she didn't acknowledge me. Instead, she snickered a little after one of her friends whispered a joke I assumed was about me. I settled for a seat closer to the door to save myself from any more humiliation. But of course, the teacher announced the new girl in town, allowing everyone to enjoy another round of stares and giggles.

The girl in front of me turned around and introduced herself. Surprisingly, it was my cousin's best friend. *Thank God*, I thought, *some relief*. She was nice and soft-spoken, and she warned me to stay away from certain crowds. I nodded and thanked her for the tips.

I quickly escaped to the bathroom in the middle of switching classes because I didn't want to risk everyone staring at me, raising my hand to ask to be excused in the middle of class. I tried to avoid as many stares and laughs as possible. Unfortunately, several girls came in before I flushed the toilet, so I stayed in the stall to avoid any awkward socialization.

"Did you see the new girl today?"

"Yeah, what was she wearing?"

"I was thinking more about her hair!"

They all laughed.

"What was wrong with it?"

I recognized it was Jena talking then. She was with the girls she sat by in class.

"Are you kidding me? She needed a brush. Her hair was frizzy; she was wearing short jeans that fit loose."

"She looks like she hasn't combed her hair in days!" another girl said. "I heard someone say she was related to Natalie."

"That's odd; Natalie looks so normal."

Immediately, humiliation punished me for staying in the stall. Had I walked out earlier, I could have avoided hearing what they thought of me. But because I stayed, I'd be repeating their words in my head as I walked around or when everyone was staring at me.

Old feelings of being an outcast hovered over me like a dark cloud. Rage was becoming a regular companion. Here, in a different state and far away from home, I was still teased about how different I looked. *Normal?* I remembered the words she said and repeated them slowly, trying to understand *normal.*

My cousin Natalie must have looked "normal" to those girls, and I guess I didn't because my hair was dark, bushy, and curly. Natalie's hair was sandy-brown, soft and her curls were loose. My freckles were dark and scattered about my face. Her light brown freckles matched her hair. Dark circles hung under my light brown eyes, but her hazel eyes perfectly matched her hair, freckles, and fair tone. My darker tone matched my darker features. I felt trapped inside my own skin, suffocated by my "abnormal" features. Looking in the mirror felt so uncomfortable because I knew nothing could be done to change who I was.

Later on at home, pretending the day was awesome came easily because I had become used to acting like everything was fine. I didn't want to worry my mom, so as much as feeling left out made me sad, I just tried to ignore it. The whispers, snickers and stares all began to feel normal as if it would be the story of my life. Eventually, I reassured myself that ignoring it every day would make the shame disappear. It worked for a little while until things started to get physical.

One day in homeroom, my usual seat next to my cousin's best friend was taken, so I decided to just take a seat in the middle of the classroom. By this time, the snickering had stopped. It was the third week of school, so the joke must've gotten old.

My teacher, a middle-aged man, was in the beginning stages of developing a beer belly. The sides of his face were always red, and beads of sweat dotted his forehead, never seeming to drip off. His voice was dry but loud enough that we wouldn't fall asleep.

He gave us empty maps of the United States and told us to fill them in for homework. "I'll be quizzing you next week, so be sure to study." He always sounded as if he had just run a mile, but he spent most of the day sitting in reality. Some of my classmates took turns asking questions, but I couldn't pay attention because the person behind me kept kicking my chair.

"Quit it!" I scowled as I spun around with my arms crossed like a pouting toddler. Jackson was a well-known bully. He taunted everyone and spent most days in the principal's office. I attempted to stand but was forced back down after Jackson yanked my braid when the bell rang. He and the rest of the class burst into laughter. Frustration got the best of me as my ears grew hot and a knot formed in my stomach. Once again, I stood up to head for the end of the line, where everyone waited for the second bell. Jackson stuck his foot out at the last minute, causing me to trip and drop all of my things. My face smacked the floor, and everyone laughed again. That was it! I was tired of being embarrassed.

I got up, drew my arm behind me, and then swung forward, landing a punch on Jackson's pale, white cheek. I didn't hold back when he pushed me, using all of my strength to push him until he fell over two desks behind him. The teacher then yanked my arm and pulled me out of the classroom. Instead of the teacher bringing us both to the principal's office, he only took me for what he explained as "aggressive behavior." Looking back, I remember that one other boy and I were the only Black students in the class. Now it's clear that sending me alone to the office perpetuated the racism I was already battling.

We entered through a heavy brown door that led to a small waiting room with only three chairs. My teacher gestured for me to take a seat as he knocked on the door and entered after the second knock. I sat there alone, daydreaming and wishing we had never moved there.

After a few moments, the teacher walked out, and the principal called me in. She asked what happened, and I decided to tell her the things that had been going on. She didn't look concerned at all. She looked like she didn't believe me.

"Look, Ariel, I don't know what happens back where you come from, but we don't do that here. Fighting is not tolerated. Expectations of good behavior are high here."

"Didn't you hear what he did to me? I was defending myself!" I replied.

"Kids tease one another, especially when they feel someone is different from them, but it's still not a reason to behave like an animal!" Her tone revealed her frustration, but she instantly looked regretful about what she said.

"Different? Animal?" I asked.

She tilted her head, looking at me from head to toe. Then, before escorting me out, she sighed and said, "I'm sure you see the difference."

Then it was clear. No matter where we lived, I'd always be an outcast. I never looked *regular* or *pure* enough for anyone. Being biracial divided me in so many ways. Even school staff started to separate me from the other kids. It is never easy to be an outcast, but it is even harder being an outcast for things you cannot change. Changing from being biracial or changing my features was not possible, but I began to believe that changing certain things could help me gain more acceptance from others.

I just knew my hair had to be the root of my problems. It was thick and uncontrollable. My mom never knew how to deal with my hair because it was different from her straight hair. In fact, my mom and I had completely different looks. She was tall, ivory-complexioned with emerald green eyes that sometimes changed to ocean blue and full, straight black hair. She kept her hair dyed red or blonde. I always wondered if my mom was white; people always thought she was until she started talking. She didn't have a heavy accent, but certain words came out with an accent.

That weekend I asked my mom for a perm. She initially said no, but I begged and begged. She gave in eventually, and over the weekend, she found someone to perm my hair. I was overjoyed! No more bushy or frizzy hair. I was finally going to be able to wear my hair out and brush it in cute styles. Luckily for me, my perm was going to get done before the next school week. So, again, there I was, hoping to fit in to make myself and others more comfortable.

After the lady washed the perm out of my hair, I was eager for it to dry. It felt so silky and smooth. Halfway into drying it, something immediately felt wrong. Rubbing my hands through my hair felt lighter than air. I looked down at my hand, then my head started spinning, and my stomach felt weak at the sight of the clump of hair in my palm. I rushed to my feet and darted toward the bathroom mirror. My hair was GONE! It was super straight but stopped at my shoulders instead of my waist. It was uneven and stiff. The damage was unchangeable. It looked like the rest of my hair would crumble at the stroke of a brush. I stood there in shock, disbelief, guilt, and hatred.

How was I going to be pretty now? I was ashamed to even look at myself. I was ashamed of everything. There I was, trying to straighten my hair to fit in and look *regular*, only to look more abnormal than before. White people thought I looked odd, Hispanics took one look at my hair and disregarded my claims to be Puerto Rican, and Black people told me I was too light to be Black. Who was I then? What was I? Why couldn't I identify with anyone? These questions would haunt my thoughts for a long time.

Why Don't You Speak Spanish?!

Two months later, we left Georgia and moved back to our old neighborhood. It didn't really make a difference to me; I didn't fit in anywhere anyhow. The only things I had missed from home were the city, the lights, the noise, and how familiar things were. In Georgia, we were surrounded by silence—all you could hear were the crickets. To be completely honest, nights in Georgia made me skittish.

The best thing about moving back home was that Tyra didn't live there anymore. So when we got back, I ended up meeting Jaqueline and her family, who lived downstairs. They were Puerto Rican, and Jaqueline was the oldest of her siblings. We became best friends.

At times, I still experienced my feelings of not belonging there. Jaqueline and her siblings spoke fluent Spanish and listened to all-Spanish music. I'd listen half of the time, not knowing what they were saying. I had a lot of fun, but still, I was reminded of not knowing my native language. The first thing Jaqueline's parents ever asked me was, "¿Hablas español?" Telling them that I didn't speak Spanish felt empty and shameful. It made me want to hide, especially when the question, "Why?" followed. I didn't know why. I just came up with answers like, "My dad is Black," because I thought it was a good excuse, but they just stared at me blankly.

Jaqueline's Quinceañera (which means sweet fifteen) was probably one of the most traumatizing experiences ever. When Jaqueline asked me to be a part of it, I felt honored because I had never been to a sweet fifteen before. I was especially excited to go because I was really young—I was only about to be eleven years old, and I was asked to be one of the fourteen girls that would be "walking out" with Jacqueline. It wasn't until the preparation time came that I started to feel out of place. You would think that since we all wore the same dress and same hairstyle, excluding the main girl herself, that I'd be comfortable, but I wasn't.

When it was time to sit in the chair to get my hair done, all the girls stared at how different my hair was. Some of them giggled when the Puerto Rican stylist struggled to part my hair and explained that the gel they were using didn't work for my hair. That was one of the worst feelings. I wanted to cry in humiliation as all the girls walked past me with their silky-smooth hair neatly done with flat twists into a bun with not a strand out of place.

I went to the bathroom and stared into the mirror, hating what I saw looking back at me. My eyes were big, round, and had that stupid dark tint underneath them. My brown freckles spread about the center of my face, my eyebrows were dark and thick, and my hair matched. My baby hair had already shriveled into curls and frizzed from the humidity. I silently cried as I thought of walking through the beautiful rented hall. It would be yet another embarrassing moment, where I'd be reminded again of how different I looked—the odd one in the crowd.

As I walked out of the bathroom, another girl was looking at herself in the mirror. She didn't have the same dress on, though. She was Jaqueline's godsister. Her dress was silver, and she, too, wore her hair in flat twists, but her curls fell to the middle of her back. She had jet black hair that appeared smooth and bouncy. No one else was around, so I questioned where everyone was. She explained that they all went to the limo and we'd be driving to the cathedral soon. My appearance shocked her when she turned around, but she quickly changed her expression, realizing she didn't hide it well.

"Are you one of the girls too?" I asked to make conversation and distract myself from her initial expression.

"Yes," she replied, her smile bright and confident. I envied her confidence.

"How come your dress is different?" I asked.

"Well, because I'm the favorite." She saw my confusion and continued, "Within the 14 girls you have, there's always a favorite. Your favorite is usually someone you're closest to." Again, I was confused. Jaqueline and I shared all of our secrets and spent every day together. We went to many places together and, on sleepovers, got yelled at for laughing way too loud. Her godsister, who was always saying bad things about Jacky, barely came over, and they always were in screaming matches when she did come over.

"Oh." My tone was low but unphased. I tried to sound content with the fact that Jacky chose someone else over me. Maybe we weren't as close as I thought.

"Ariel, right?"

"Yes," I replied in slight shock but with a hint of pride because she knew my name. Then she started to explain as if I asked, or she read my body language.

"Yeah, you were the one Jaqueline wanted to be her favorite." Her tone and smirk gave me an unpleasant vibe. "I'm sure you know why her mom said no."

"Her mom likes me, so I have no idea what you're talking about," I snapped back.

"It has nothing to do with liking you!" She rolled her eyes. "A Quinceañera is about culture. Her family from Puerto Rico will be coming, and her mom and dad wanted everything and everyone to be perfect," she said as she looked in the mirror, signaling that she was perfect. "You don't look Hispanic, at least not Puerto Rican, your hair is always out of control, and you don't even SPEAK SPANISH!" Her words felt like a knife, scrapping me as she pointed out my flaws.

"Look, I'm sorry, but we should go. Forget I said anything," she suddenly said.

Forget? How was something like that supposed to be forgotten? A wave of hatred came over me. I thought my chest was going to burst from the rage I felt. A knock at the door startled me, and I wiped my face quickly. It took all the strength in my bones to keep from breaking the mirror just to stop my image from looking back at me. Dashing out of the room prevented me from even seeing who was at the door. As I was running to the car, Jacky's real sister stopped me. She explained that she was in the room getting dressed and heard everything that had happened.

"I'm so sorry she said those things. She's always like that to us," she said. Listening to her, all I could think about was what the god-sister told me. "Anyway, I told Jaqueline what she said, and she feels terrible and never wanted you to be hurt. She was so sad she said those things about you. If you want, Jacky can explain to the stylist that you should have a different style and shouldn't have to wear it if it doesn't agree with your hair texture."

"Texture?" I asked.

"Yeah, it's different from ours. So, Jacky found another style she thinks looks perfect for you."

Although I felt a little better that Jacky stuck up for me, it still bothered me that I had to deal with constantly being treated differently in some way. Also, Jacky was older than me, so she always felt the need to protect me.

Night came quickly, and I felt better after my hair was fixed. They used a different gel that I recommended. I learned what worked from my aunt, who kept my hair braided for most of my younger years. I thought of not even going at that point, but I didn't want to let my best friend down. So I sat alone most of the night at a corner table where no one could see me, trying to hide my shame and guilt of not knowing my native language once again.

I couldn't tell whether this situation made me feel better or worse than the time my third grade teacher, Ms. Rodriguez, asked me to read a sentence aloud in Spanish. Those situations made me feel isolated from my own people. They never made me feel accepted. Growing older, I felt uncomfortable around Hispanic crowds and honestly attempted to avoid them, especially once my best friend moved away. None of my friends were Hispanic then, not because I didn't want Hispanic friends, but because they didn't accept me.

STAGE TWO: ANGER

My mom used to tell me my hair was fine, but part of me always felt like she didn't understand because her hair was considered "acceptable" by others. My aunt did my hair in braids for most of my childhood, and she was the type that felt like kids shouldn't question adults. For me, my hair wasn't a question; I was just trying to explain how I wanted to understand myself.

There was a time my mom picked me up from school, and I was all over the place. People were making fun of my hair because it was in braids, and they were telling me, "You swear you're Black—white people always wanna be down." I was upset and crying. I remember my cousins were all picking on me and my hair the night before because the comb broke while my aunt was combing it, and I finally told my mom it wasn't fair that I was half Black and different from all of them. The lecture my aunt gave me was one I'd never forget. She said, "You should never be ashamed of who you are. Just because your hair is different doesn't mean you should hate it. I like doing your hair because there are so many styles your hair can take. You have thick hair, and it's versatile. So why would you be ashamed to be mixed? You have the best of both worlds and can share history from two different races. You should love that."

I knew I couldn't change my hair, which was why I was so angry. When she said I had the best of both worlds, I just couldn't see it. As a child, having thick hair and bushy eyebrows wasn't beautiful. People called my mom beautiful all the time; my cousins too. I envied their looks. Their thin eyebrows. Their hair that flowed in the wind while mine didn't.

My animosity just built up over the years as I struggled to deal with my hair. It agitated me as I tried straightening it or wetting it so it could curl up. Nothing worked! My hair would still frizz up, and my curls would turn into a huge afro. Shaving my head bald was a thought on many occasions.

Learning My Hair in High School

In high school, I attempted to make friends with a group of Puerto Rican girls. We hung out almost every day, had slumber parties, and did girly things together, like get our nails and hair done. It was going well until one day, one of the girls and I had a dispute, which resulted in them jumping me. One of them yelled, "You're not one of us!" The only difference between them and me was that I didn't speak Spanish, and I was biracial. At that point, I felt maybe they were right; it was silly to think they'd actually be friends with me. What hurt the most was that two of the girls and I had known each other for a long time because we went to grade school together. It was then that I completely isolated myself from Hispanic girls. To them, I was an outsider.

Reuniting with my god sisters was a huge turning point for me. They guided me and helped me learn about myself in ways my mom's side of the family couldn't. I'm not saying my mom didn't want to or didn't try, but I kept to myself a lot, mostly because I felt she wouldn't understand.

My god sisters Laura and Reina started showing me the dos and don'ts. One time, my older godsister Laura told me, "Girl, you Black; you can't use this type of gel. Your hair is too thick, and it won't hold." She then started to show me the gel I should use. She used to put my hair in different styles that were better for my hair, and I really enjoyed them. The hairstyles were more girly, and I didn't have to wear my whole head in cornrows. She'd put my hair in ponytails with extensions or braid it into a bun or ponytail. Laura was very blunt, but it made me feel better. Those moments meant a lot because I didn't have an older sister, let alone one who could identify with my struggles.

Although I was learning my hair, struggles still found me. Once I started to wear extensions, people picked on me more. One of the first times I wore a ponytail extension, a girl picked on me so badly that I took the style out. I was in front of my building, and some girls came over from across the street to play like they usually did. As we were playing, one of the girls just burst out into laughter. While my god sister Reina and I were confused and just staring at them, the other girls seemed to be in on the joke. At that point, we knew the joke was about us. Then one of them said, "How you Spanish with a ponytail piece?" The back of my ears turned red, and my cheeks blushed from embarrassment. I was so mad that I felt like I could hear my heart beating.

Reina called the same week, and we talked about the incident. She understood me and how I felt, but she responded that I shouldn't be ashamed to wear my hair in any style. Although I knew that was true, it didn't make me feel any better.

It took a couple of months before I actually tried to come to terms with my hair and the fact that it couldn't be changed. Both Laura and Reina felt I was insecure about my looks and hair. Laura ended up getting in contact with my mother and explained what my hair needed since I was growing up. She told her I was growing out of the cornrows and four ponytail stage, and thank God she did.

That weekend, Laura and Reina ended up taking me to a salon. That was my first time being in one, and my confusion was obvious when Laura asked, "Do you know what to get?" Since I didn't know what to ask for, Laura walked up to the counter and told the lady, "Give her a doobie and blow the roots out, no perm because she's trying to nurse her hair back to health." I was amazed by their back and forth exchange, thinking, *dang, she knew exactly what to do. Where was Laura all my life, and what was a doobie?*

An hour later, I found out, and boy was I ecstatic! My hair was straight and wrapped in bobby pins. I was so anxious to find out what it would look like when the pins came out. Afterward, we visited a beauty supply store, and of course, I was lost. Laura said, "You're going to love this place."

"Why?" I asked.

"Everything you'll ever need for your hair will be here," Laura replied.

"Really? They have a whole store for my hair type?"

Laura stared at me, puzzled. I could tell she felt bad for me. When we got there, I saw what she meant. Even today, the beauty supply store is one of my favorite places to be. There were different types of gel, hair straighteners, and hair grease. And there were girls on the front of spray bottles and shampoos who looked like me. We picked up a silk scarf and a doobie brush, and the rest was history. Finally,

I knew a store I could visit to find the products that worked best for me. I was comfortable in there and didn't feel like I was being judged.

So yes, I figured out how to tame my hair and later how to do it on my own. But did this make me entirely happy? The answer was no. Even though I thought my hair was going to solve all my problems, it didn't. I was still bullied about wanting to be Black and not looking Hispanic.

When did it stop? Honestly never. Still today, people ask me, "Why don't you speak Spanish?" or "Why do you wear your hair like a Black girl?" However, it stopped phasing me a bit in high school.

I can't pretend I wasn't a nervous wreck on the first day of high school. But I must say, I was way more confident knowing I'd be with real friends. That was the only thing that calmed my nerves. I felt like a new person; my hair was different, and I was growing into my own look and style. Having friends who accepted me and didn't let my ethnicity play a role in our friendship comforted me. They didn't expect me to be or look a certain way. Instead, they embraced me and the fact that I was biracial. Acceptance amongst others was all that I needed, and they not only accepted me but also respected me and encouraged me to embrace my roots.

I highlight this moment because it was one of the first times I felt accepted and not isolated because of my ethnicity. I wore a sew-in with long hair extensions, and my friends didn't judge me; instead, they complimented me and encouraged me. They made me feel welcomed and helped me understand my culture, which I didn't have before.

High school was more comfortable. I felt like a weight was lifted off my shoulders because, for once, I wasn't being stared at or questioned about my looks or my hair. No one cared, or so I thought!

Although I felt more comfortable with myself at that time, I became increasingly angry during the last two years of high school. It became a part of who I was. My friends and I were always fighting. The girls would say things like, "Puerto Ricans can't fight; they're punks." One time a girl told her friend, "Smack that white girl because I don't like her." The smack never happened, by the way. By then, I was always ready to defend myself. I had to defend myself because I was Hispanic, and I looked more Hispanic than Black. My other friends weren't teased as much as I was. People didn't say things to them like they did to me or do things to them that they did to me.

I remember a girl told me, "They are always going to pick on you because you're Puerto Rican, and everyone says Puerto Ricans can't fight well." Having to defend myself from bullies, yes, almost all kids dealt with it. But having to defend myself over something I couldn't change was devastating. I couldn't change being Hispanic or my complexion. People didn't believe I was Black because of my complexion, and I knew that was their issue because of how people would react when I said I was half Black. They'd say, "You're mad light; I just thought you were Puerto Rican," or "You don't look Black."

It's horrifying to think about because honestly, what does being Black look like? Or why does being Puerto Rican have to look a certain way? I never wore my hair curly, mostly because I couldn't. I did not know at the time that there were products for my hair to define my curls. Every time I'd say I didn't know what to do with my hair, I'd get the same reply: "Why don't you just wet it and put gel on it and wear it curly?" The answer was that *I freaking couldn't.* I always found that comment so prejudiced because people wouldn't say that to someone of any other ethnicity. They wouldn't tell an Indian girl or an Asian girl to do that—am I right? So just because I was Hispanic, I had to curl and gel my hair? Prejudiced comments against any race always annoyed me. Like when Hispanic guys would ask me why I wore my hair in braids or put weave in, they didn't like that it made me look more Black. I never understood why it mattered. Not only that, but what the heck was wrong with looking Black?!

Of course, boys came into the picture as I grew older and moved through high school. One thing that stood out to me was how guys would say something like, "I love Spanish women." I was quick to tell them I was half Black; I never hid it. Sometimes people wouldn't even know I was Hispanic and assumed I was one hundred percent Black, but I always corrected them. The most unsettling and insulting thing was that numerous guys were saying, "I like you because you're Puerto Rican, and I love Puerto Rican girls." When guys said that, it didn't flatter me; it was an insult. I'm not only Puerto Rican and I'm not only Black, I am biracial and my race should not have an effect on whether a guy liked me or not. I leaned away from guys who would date me based on race. I found it a little disturbing the way boys thought about race. It seemed like it played a major part in what was important when dating a woman.

One thing I always regretted in high school was having the choice of whether to take French or Spanish class. I chose French. When people asked, "Why French instead of Spanish?" I told them that I could always learn Spanish from my family, whereas French, I couldn't. But that was just a cover-up because I didn't want to hear, "So much for a native speaker," or if not that, it would be something like, "Aren't you Spanish?" I just didn't want to face that. Truth is, I was embarrassed not to know my native language.

I Didn't Date Hispanic Guys

I know what you're thinking. Why not date within my race? Or that's racist, *blah blah blah*. Let me explain. Growing up, Hispanic guys always turned me down. This goes back to my preteen and teenage years. My friends were always big on the Spanish guys where I lived. They believed they were so cute, but I disagreed. I always expressed to my friends that I didn't date Hispanic guys.

It was never because "Oh, they're Hispanic, so they aren't my type." It was more so because they never accepted me. In their eyes, I wasn't "truly Puerto Rican" because I didn't speak Spanish. And to top it off, I didn't have the ideal look of a Puerto Rican woman. What they looked for and accepted, I didn't have. I didn't have the long, straight hair or the long, curly hair that you could wet, gel, and stay that way for hours. I didn't have the bangs. And this is not what I'm assuming! These things were said to me, or a friend would come back and tell me what a guy said. I was once told by a Hispanic man in my early teens that "Black girls are great to have fun with and fool around with, but I wouldn't ever make one my serious girlfriend or wife." Hearing that felt like a stab in my heart. *His words permanently damaged me.* Although he was not speaking of me, I felt like it was a jab at my culture and people. He left a permanent scar on me that took years to heal. Not even my best cocoa butter or aloe could get rid of it.

I once dated a guy who was biracial like me. At first, we really hit it off. Comfort hugged me when we were around each other because he didn't judge me for not speaking my native language. But it all ended one day when he said to me in a disgusted tone, "Why do you keep braids in your hair? You look like a Morena."

Although I'm half-Black, that still offended me. So I asked him, "What's wrong with looking Black? Am I not as attractive when I look Black? Because regardless of your reasoning, I am Black." He couldn't answer me. I expected it was because he knew there was no way to respond without sounding racist or prejudiced.

Comments and conversations like that always killed me inside. A friend once told me something that made my heart ache with sadness because it was reality. She said, "In America, when people look at you, and they think you're too pretty, they assume you're mixed as if you cannot be entirely Black and still beautiful."

When she said this, my heart sank because, for one, it was the reality of what many people think in America, and two, it was something I always felt but could never put into words. Small comments can still have a huge effect on someone, so always be careful. That person may already be suffering in silence. I know because I was one of those people.

So again, I went through my adolescent years and young adult years, staying away from Hispanic men altogether. I just didn't want to feel that hurt, and honestly, what they said and thought about me—I already felt like that about myself. I didn't want to be reminded that I didn't speak my native language because it was already a sensitive topic. But, most importantly, it infuriated me because I hated the constant rejection from my own people.

Anger quickly turned into bargaining because I didn't understand who I was. A lot of what I went through was due to men not accepting me or being an outcast altogether. Part of my struggle with identity was connected to not being in touch with my dad so he could teach me the important history behind who I was. When you're not biracial, it's easier to identify yourself, especially when you have parents around who share that identity. I'm not saying my mom wasn't there for me; I'm saying that also I needed my dad to help me understand who part of me was. And not knowing who I was led me to a confusing struggle with my identity.

STAGE THREE: BARGAINING

My early twenties were rough. I was always jumping from job to job, trying to learn my likes and dislikes. I always had a job, but I was either bored or felt like it wasn't a good fit. One of my favorite jobs was at the airport. It was always busy, and I met new people, including famous ones, and there were a lot of perks to the job. I worked in a fancy restaurant and enjoyed the way they used technology in their style of service. It was all such a rush.

I'm bringing this up for one reason and one reason only. I met someone. Not just anyone, but someone who completely consumed me. Yes, it was a man, but to me, he wasn't just any man—he was the man who made me feel like, *Oh my God, he's THE man*. He was such a gentleman; never disrespectful, polite, and amazing at his job. Whenever someone important came to the restaurant, the bosses would choose him to provide them with excellent service. He was pretty impressive and highly articulate. He was one to work hard, and the bosses bragged about him.

I remember distinctly when they opened a new restaurant which was a huge deal; it was all the big boss could talk about. They opened it right across from where I worked. At first, there was only to be one person to work the eight tables. Who do you think they chose?

Meeting this guy was a key point in my life for a couple of reasons. One, he made me realize what type of man I wanted. Two, he was inspiring. He was the type that always knew the answer to what I thought was the hardest question, but he wasn't arrogant; he just humbly taught people. Three, he had the type of manners that made me question mine. He was very gentle but manly. He didn't let people walk all over him; he always kept his composure, and that was amazing. Seems amazing, right? What could possibly go wrong?

He and I always had conversations during our downtime. There were televisions across from our restaurant, so we'd always watch the news together and talk about what was happening. I remember asking him something about politics, and he broke it down to a point where I thought, *Wow, he's pretty impressive.* It was hard to believe he was younger than I was. Over time, we got to know each other more and more. We discovered that we both liked to read. Whenever I finished a book, I'd talk to him about it. He listened tentatively, and then he'd talk about what he read.

On one of my routine trips to the bookstore, I told myself I would venture out and stop reading only one genre. History always intrigued me, no matter what period it was. Astronomy was intriguing to me too. But the moment when I picked up a book about Ancient Greek Mythology was unforgettable. I was so excited because I didn't know much about it and was eager to learn.

At work the next day, I was so happy to share my new book with him. I told him about it and thought he was going to be fascinated, but he stared at me blankly and lashed out, "You need to learn your own culture before you read about someone else's!" My heart shattered into pieces. Devastated wasn't even the word to describe what I felt. The feeling of my heart sinking into my stomach hung over me like a dark cloud. It took everything in me to keep from balling my eyes out. I couldn't believe he said that to me. I didn't even think someone could say something like that to me. I was beyond humiliated, but I never expressed to him the damage he caused.

After that experience, I battled with myself about so many things. I began to feel like it was my fault that I didn't speak Spanish. I should've tried harder to learn it. I knew where my mom's side of the family came from because I always asked my grandmother, but guilt got the best of me. Maybe people were right to call me out for not knowing my own language.

Not only did I beat myself up about my inability to speak fluent Spanish, but contemplating earlier decisions I made, like getting that perm in my hair that made it fall out, started to haunt me again. It haunted me after the book incident because it made me think that my hair would still have its natural pattern had I not gotten the perm. Maybe if I hadn't put it in my hair, I'd look more Hispanic. I drooled over that guy and secretly felt that he never accepted me because I didn't look Hispanic enough and didn't know my native language. He seemed to click with the other girls we worked with who were Hispanic. They all resembled one another with their long straight or curly hair, spoke fluent Spanish, and were what most guys considered beautiful.

I was kind of jealous of those girls in a way, not because of their looks, but because they had his attention over how they looked and their ability to speak their native language. I was jealous because I secretly hated myself but couldn't change it. I knew if I'd at least spoken Spanish, he would've never said what he said to me, and then he and other people would accept me. What was even more humiliating for me was that he was also from the islands, spoke his native Caribbean language, and was very culture-driven, so I couldn't even say anything.

There was this one girl who he seemed to gush over, and I'll never forget it. She was Columbian and extremely beautiful with waist-length straight but bouncy chocolate-colored hair, ivory complexion, and brown eyes. She had an accent when she spoke English, and she was a very funny and sweet girl. But, of course, she spoke fluent Spanish, and it honestly broke my heart. I felt ashamed of myself. I felt like I wasn't beautiful enough for him or anyone else in many ways because my hair didn't look like hers. Mine was short, dark, and thick. I wore it out straight, and it was shoulder length. Most of the time, I put in extensions and wore false lashes. I remember going to the bathroom at work and shedding tears because I felt rejected, unwanted and unattractive. The mirror became a permanent enemy of mine for a long time after that.

One day when I returned home from work, I told my grandmother I wanted to learn Spanish. She looked at me and said, "You already know the basics; you just need to learn how to hold a conversation. You can only do that by trying." And she was right. I always felt self-conscious speaking Spanish because it wasn't my first language. I'd had instances where I knew exactly what the person was saying but responded in English. Trying to speak Spanish would always bring me back to my Spanish teacher saying, "So much for a native speaker." That, along with many other comments, haunted me. The only words I would say in Spanish were those I secretly couldn't say in English growing up or couldn't explain in English. Like, how do you explain pasteles? Or sigue?

STAGE FOUR: DEPRESSION

Would you believe that guy's comments made me fall into a deep depression no one knew about? I was in my twenties, yet trauma from my childhood began to haunt me again. I was so disappointed in myself. For a while, I didn't date anyone else, and when I did, I made sure to stay away from men who questioned me about my ethnicity when we first met. It was crazy that it was the mid-2000s, and I was dealing with racism, bigotry and prejudiced comments. Not only that but I was being rejected based on how "Hispanic" I was or not being "Black enough."

While completing my undergraduate degree, I met a guy. We liked each other a lot and went on dates. The only problem was he'd given me weird energy as though he was holding back a little. I noticed that whenever I went to his house, we went straight to his room. Never saw any of his relatives. When I finally got up the courage to ask him about it, he told me, "My parents would never approve because you're Hispanic." He came from a culture where they had to date and marry within their race. It didn't even matter if I spoke my native language, and in fact, it probably would've made it worse. *Foolish*, I thought to myself, because in my heart, I believed I'd always have to deal with this and would never be able to be whole.

Being biracial in my early and mid-twenties took a toll on me, mainly because I tried so hard to understand myself. It affected me on many levels because I never felt like I fit in regardless of who I was around. There was never a time when I was in a group, and other biracial girls or guys were there. I was either the only Hispanic girl there or the only Black girl there. I was always uncomfortable in my own skin. This made me separate myself and stopped me from going out with friends and mingling with others.

During this time, something stood out to me that many people overlooked. Whenever I filled out job applications, a survey or anything asking me to identify myself, there was no place for me. This is what survey questions or job application answers looked like:

Question: What's your race/ethnic background?

- **American Indian/Alaska Native (not Hispanic or Latino)**
- **Asian (not Hispanic or Latino)**
- **Black/African American (not Hispanic or Latino)**
- **Hispanic or Latino**
- **Two or more races (not Hispanic or Latino)**
- **Native Hawaiian (not Hispanic or Latino)**
- **White (not Hispanic or Latino)**
- **I choose not to identify**

This always affected the day I was having for the worse. Not only was there no option for being biracial, but there was also no option to be both Hispanic and another race. Even next to the two or more races option, it said: "not Hispanic or Latino." That frustrated me. I disliked the way society as a whole always made me feel like I had to choose one, and because my skin tone was light, I was forced to identify as Hispanic and sometimes even white. Going forward, this needs to change. Biracial individuals have a right to identify with two races or more. We shouldn't have to choose one. When we are forced to choose one, it's basically making us feel like we can only be proud to be one race.

I never realized how much my identity crisis affected me. I needed a lot of time alone to understand myself, but it was difficult because I had no one I could identify with. Loving myself should have come easily, but it didn't. It wasn't until years later that I realized it was an issue that needed more attention and healing.

My son Kaiden was born in 2012. It was truly magical to have a mini-me. I wouldn't say I went through postpartum depression because instead of depression, I experienced separation anxiety more than anything else. I wouldn't let him go anywhere for the first year. I was terrified. I remember Reina finally forcing me out of the house when my son was around four months old. I was so afraid. The whole time I was at the movies, I was texting Reina and my grandmother to the point that they turned their phones off. I was just over-protective and wanted to know his every move.

This worsened as he got older because I knew questions would soon come. I cried so hard when he turned three years old, and I took him to school for the first time. Leaving him for seven hours was so huge for me. I was worried about everything—wondering if he was being mistreated or if he was scared. Thankfully, I had a friend who was dropping off her son too, and they were in the same class. She definitely helped me through the process. While I held back tears, she didn't, and because she knew me she knew how afraid I was.

She told me it was okay to cry and show how emotional this major milestone was.

My son was truly amazing in every way. It wasn't until he reached kindergarten that things started to get a little challenging. On the first day of school, the principal wanted to talk to my son's parents about his summer packet. He was attending a no-nonsense type of school, and they wanted to discuss how I could help Kaiden with his workload. When I got there, I was waiting alongside another parent. The principal looked past me and said, "We will see you for Kaiden now," and I was both shocked and hurt. I then stepped up and said, "Kaiden is my child."

Kaiden was several shades darker than I was because his dad had darker skin. As a result, people always expected Kaiden to be someone else's child. No matter who I was with, if they were darker in complexion, strangers would look past me, saying to my friends, "Aww, your son is cute," or "Aww, whose baby?" if I was alone. It had a lot to do with Kaiden not understanding why he was darker than I was and his feeling like he didn't belong with me.

One day he came from school and told me, "I'm not Puerto Rican; only you're Puerto Rican because you're yellow and I'm brown." It was heartbreaking. I understood that he was only about five or six years old, but it bothered me because I felt that struggling with knowing who he was could be the start of self-hate.

Another time he asked me, "Why don't I speak Spanish if I'm Puerto Rican?" And it made me feel so foolish. I tried explaining that he didn't have to speak Spanish to be Puerto Rican, but then he said, "I'm Jamaican, not Puerto Rican." When I asked him who told him that, he said, "At my school, they said I look Jamaican, not Puerto Rican." That made me upset. Why would they tell him that?

He was partially Jamaican, but that didn't mean he couldn't also be Puerto Rican. I felt like he was reliving my same pain.

When Kaiden was in second grade, I decided to take him to counseling because I knew how difficult it was not to understand being biracial. Honestly, I was still battling it myself but wanted to help him in ways I never was. The first day we saw the counselor, my son had a meltdown. He was saying things like, "I'm dark brown, which means I'm stupid. Me and my mom are not supposed to be together because of our skin! She's white; I'm brown! I'm supposed to be in the back of the bus." My poor child learned about slavery and the civil rights movement in school and couldn't handle it. I was upset because I felt like maybe he was too young to hear about that. He needed to learn where our people came from and not only the tragic things that happened to us. We are so much more than slaves! His learning had to start with me! I needed to find a way to educate myself, so I did. I went back to school and began searching for OUR identity.

STAGE FIVE: ACCEPTANCE

Kaiden and I were in the middle of a conversation when he said again, "Mommy, I'm not a Puerto Rican because I don't speak Spanish." Again, it hurt me that he felt like that because whether he knew it or not, we shouldn't have been outcasts because we didn't speak Spanish. I wanted him to be proud of his background. But for him to be proud, I had to be proud, inside and out. I had to stop being embarrassed about not knowing the language and be proud regardless of how anyone felt because the truth was, I loved being Puerto Rican and Black. People around me made me feel like I couldn't be proud to be both or that I had to choose one to look like or be like or act like. That wasn't fair, and what's worse, I allowed it for so long just to make others around me comfortable and to avoid feeling ashamed.

Research became my best friend. Reading about where I came from soothed me. In college, I had the opportunity to learn about where I came from, thanks to a history class. We began to learn about natives, and my professor started talking about Tainos. That rang a bell. We visited my Tia once, my grandmother's sister, and she spoke of doing an ancestry test. She spoke of her grandmother's features, saying we came from a background of Africans and Tainos. Hearing my professor talk about Taino people felt like a calling.

So, I did the research and found myself smiling and loving what I learned. Learning of them explained why my great grandmother was of bronze complexion, with long, dark flowing hair and strong cheekbones. Her house reminded me of an old cabin and had a unique antique look. She ate with wooden spoons and bowls and drank out of recycled aluminum cans. We came from strong people. They were kind people who worshiped through dance and were spiritual. They believed in the stars, which I believe explained why I always loved to look at the stars. Something told me it was already embedded in me. Taino meant good and noble. I also learned that Tainos inhabited most Caribbean islands, which back then were referred to as Hispaniola.

I didn't indulge in my Taino heritage only. My dad's side mattered big time! My African roots would always be with me. It was harder to know which part of Africa my dad's side was from because they were born in America. Still, his side mattered. Finding my dad's side of the family would take time since he couldn't be around as much due to his difficult upbringing. I did, however, have three older cousins and an aunt on his side who always made me feel welcomed. They always complimented me. My older cousin Tisa was always an inspiration because she was a Black woman who spoke Spanish and wasn't afraid to. She made me realize a language can be someone's native tongue, but no specific race owns it. Meaning anyone can learn, regardless of their background. She always made me feel comfortable with my hair, wearing different styles and embracing my African roots. Self-acceptance was coming, and I loved it.

I continued to search for myself because I needed to know who I was and wanted to understand, so I finally got up the courage to do it: an ancestry trace. I was completely overwhelmed with my results as well as my son's. We had an extremely high percentage of ancestry from Nigeria. We were also matched with other regions in Africa. The results traced us to the Caribbean region, more specifically Puerto Rico and the other islands. It was unbelievable to see my son's excitement. He was intrigued, and I was just proud to understand ALL of me finally.

Finally Coming Full Circle

When I was younger, hearing Spanish music for the first time forced me to plunge my fingers into my ears. The trumpets blasted through the speakers like a marching band was right there in the living room. Reminiscing, I'm ashamed to say I covered my ears, but I didn't cover my ears because of the type of music it was. It was because it was so loud and unexpected. A friend of my grandmother, who we considered like family, marched over to me, grabbed my hands, and shoved my fingers down, away from my ears. Then, in Spanish, she asked me, "Why are you covering your ears? This is your music—embrace it!" Before I knew it, she stood me up and yelled through the music, "Escucha; listen!" The drums forced me to tap my thighs in unison with the beat. I couldn't deny how the drums made me feel. I wanted to dance but didn't know how and didn't want to look stupid.

Sometimes at home, I'd practice alone in the bathroom where no one could see me. Growing up, learning how to dance to Spanish music meant a lot to my family. My uncles and other family members would turn on bachata and grab whoever was sitting down. Those were moments I remember feeling proud because I wasn't judged. They taught me and enjoyed teaching me. I fell in love with bachata music.

Years later, no one knew I could dance to Spanish music; I hid it from everyone. I didn't dance around my friends, and although I shouldn't have been ashamed to, I was. Listening to Spanish music was hard when people would say things like, "Girl, you don't even know what they are saying." It was partially true. Still, it shouldn't have mattered.

One summer in my late twenties, I met this amazing Puerto Rican family from Brooklyn. They had two sons and recently moved to New Jersey. I'm mentioning them for two reasons. One, they never judged me for not knowing Spanish, and two, I identified with their sons because they were Puerto Rican and didn't speak Spanish. They made me feel so much better confiding in them about not knowing the language. They'd offer to give me tips on certain Hispanic dishes I didn't know how to cook. If I didn't know what a word meant, they'd tell me, and they taught me how to dance salsa. I remember going home, turning on the radio, putting it on the highest volume, and recording myself dancing. I was so happy and comfortable for the first time, dancing and singing to *Me Tengo Que Ir*. This family was the first Hispanic family outside of my own that accepted me and never cracked jokes. I felt genuinely comfortable.

They taught me that it was okay to love my heritage and ethnicity still because who I was wasn't defined by it. The way I wear my hair doesn't make me less or more of anything. I didn't get absurd looks when I wore my eyelash extensions, hair extensions, or protective styles. Their family came with many shades of skin, many hair textures, and even many accents, which I loved.

It was then I realized that Hispanics come in different shades, different sizes, and backgrounds. I shouldn't allow pressure from others telling me what I should and should not act like based on my race. Self-love is important. That family really helped on my journey to self-love. After my journey with them, I realized that maybe most of my hurt or isolation came from not having anyone around me who was biracial. Real healing and acceptance came from meeting other biracial women and men.

What You Need to Know Having a Biracial Child

Stereotypes occur continuously. Regardless of your race, someone has something to say. What happens, though, when you're more than one race? Nothing hurts more than being an outcast due to your ethnicity, but it hurts more when part of who you are rejects you. The most pain I endured came from being outcasted by my own people. This happens more often for biracial individuals than people may think.

It is already a battle within yourself to understand who you are; we shouldn't have to battle to prove ourselves regardless of who we are around. When you are biracial, others treat you like you aren't enough, and when someone says it out loud, we feel a different pain because we are divided on race. But we shouldn't have to be divided amongst people because of it.

Yes, we are biracial; still, no one should make us feel like we have to pick one race to behave like or look like. We constantly have to fight to be what we want. We want to be seen for who we are as individuals, not as a race. And I know people of all races feel like that when they are among people of different ethnicities. The problem with being biracial is how can we "behave or look like one race or ethnicity" WHEN WE AREN'T? Why should we even have to choose when we are proud of both or several ethnicities? Here are five pointers that'll help you and your biracial child process who they are.

1) Assume nothing! Understand that terms common to adults are not common to your child. For example, please do not tell your child, "you are half this and half that." From experience, I can assure you they will take this literally and assume being half-and-half is a physical trait rather than DNA and genetics passed down from their parents. I cannot express how many times I questioned my outer appearance because I was "half-and-half."

2) Create a safe place for open conversation. Ask your child if they understand what being biracial means. When they understand, be mindful that it may not be a big deal for you, but it may be a big deal for them. They may overload you with questions, or they may let it sink in. Either way, ask them what questions they may have. Always make an effort to ask them if anything is bothering them or ask what's been on their mind. Children may not always talk about things others have said to them. You never want them to have an internal battle without expressing it. They must know you are always there for them to explain what they don't understand. The last thing you want is for others to tell your child who they are and give them false information.

3) Start conversing as early in the child's life as possible. Every child is different. There is no specific age to discuss your child's ethnic background. You can discuss this with them whenever you feel they are ready. Although we shouldn't have to even bring up race as a serious conversation with our

children, sadly, we kind of have to in America. We are continuously being asked to identify our race, ethnicity, religion, and so on. As I've said before, the last thing you want is for your child to be confused or for society to tell your child who they are.

4) Research and share at an age-appropriate level. This is especially true for grade school kids. Make it fun and simple. This is the age when children love to learn new things. Research and show them you are just as interested as they are. Visit places that are related to their ancestors. Museums and historical sites are great trips to take with your children. This will allow your child to feel more connected to their background. Research is extremely important when you have a biracial kid, and the child is missing a parent. Often, children want to know more about the missing parent's background. Do not hesitate to help your child understand the missing pieces.

5) Teach pride in all of who your child is. You may believe that teaching them about one part of them is enough; it's not. No matter what race or ethnicity your biracial child is, acknowledging all parts of them is important. Be sure to show them not one part of them is better or more important. Let them know they can be proud of every part of themselves. People will try to tell them they can only be one ethnicity or race and can't show pride in more than one. This is completely false! If they want to embrace fifteen different races, they can. They will be comfortable with who they are as long as you are there to guide them.

LEARNING FROM INTERVIEWS

What follows here is a mixture of lessons I've learned throughout the years and things that I learned from meeting other biracial men and women. One realization I made is that many biracial individuals experience the same thing. While I thought my experiences were unique, many of my experiences happened to be common amongst other biracial kids, including bullying, feeling alone, or just feeling rejected altogether.

Biracial kids need support from their parents or anyone who is watching over them, no questions asked. Unfortunately, the ugly truth is a lot of parents, friends or guardians of biracial children do not know how to help them. This is a major problem. What you do not want to happen to your child is that they become consumed by peer pressure. But it's never too late to approach this the right way. What's important is that your child does not feel confused, isolated, or outcast and end up trying to be what people "think" they should be. If you do not know how to support a biracial child, that's what I'm here for. I'm about to teach you four major ways you can greatly impact your biracial child.

As I sat and interviewed two other biracial individuals, their stories began to shock me. Their interviews were held separately, and they did not know one another.

Me: Have you ever encountered anything that made you feel judged based on being biracial?

Fran: Because I am a woman who looks more Black than Hispanic and reside in an urban community, others usually expect me to have no manners. On top of that, they expect that I will be unruly. For example, I visited a doctor's office in a suburban area of New Jersey. When I entered, I was very polite, greeted the receptionist and continued with my appointment. The doctor's office was predominately White except for one Black woman. After my appointment, I again spoke to the receptionist, saying, "Thank you and have a nice day." The lady then physically showed an expression of complete shock as if it were impossible for a Black woman to be polite.

Interviewing Fran opened my eyes to the importance of reinforcement. Biracial children need someone who will tell them, "Hey, your hair is curlier or puffier because you are not only White or you are not only Hispanic. You have a darker tone because you are biracial and also Black or Jamaican," so they can understand who they are.

At one point, I believed that only biracial women went through what I went through because I rarely ran into men or young boys who identified as biracial. That all changed when I met a biracial man. We sat down, and he explained the following.

Hanif: People want you to choose one to behave like, but there's a different and deeper meaning to that. Someone saying, "Why don't you act Black," or "You're not Black because of the way you speak," actually demonstrates hate toward a specific race. Especially when it comes from a Black man or woman.

An example of what Hanif described is a Black man being upset if a biracial woman looks more Black than Hispanic. This was explained earlier in the book. A Black man asked me, "Why do you get box braids in your hair? It makes you look more Black!" This is indeed self-hate because coming from a Black man, why is it a problem for a woman to look Black or be Black? This in itself makes Black women feel like they aren't beautiful, which is problematic.

Hanif: I was actually bullied because I was biracial. I was constantly feeling hopeless and trapped, not understanding what I'd done to deserve the bullying.

Hanif's past interactions were completely relatable. One thing I could relate to more than anything was his account of the hardship of finding friends.

Hanif: I was too light to hang with the Black guys and shut out from the Hispanic community for not speaking Spanish and having different hair. This is the hardest part of being biracial because all you want is a friendship, but when you look too "different," you are always being judged. Being biracial, you are never enough for anyone. You either aren't Black enough or not Hispanic enough. As a child, that is so hard to understand and cope with. It causes so much confusion and feelings of loneliness because you want to feel like you belong, but you're always labeled an outcast. Labeled as trying to be something you aren't. You can never win with anyone. You are never enough for anyone.

Me: When it comes to being biracial, what is important to know?

Hanif: It's not about race or pigmentation; it's about culture and individualism. Culture is important, not race.

Hanif's point is so important and relevant, especially in these current times. People need to hear that race doesn't matter. No race is better than another. We are all beautiful and unique. What makes us unique is the culture we partake in. Culture is such a beautiful thing to experience. Hanif went on to share an example:

Hanif: I know of a Russian woman adopted by a Dominican family. The woman still identified herself as Russian, but I explained to her, "You speak fluent Spanish and live your everyday life by your parents' Dominican traditions, which makes you Dominican."

Me: What should parents do differently when or if they have a biracial child?

Hanif: Definitely teach your kids to love themselves regardless of how they look. This is what it all comes to—teaching them to love themselves and others based on how their heart is and not their looks.

Reflections

Dividing someone who is already biracial is difficult. We are already divided technically being biracial; we are mixed with two or more races. It causes great depression when you question yourself and who you are. People want to classify you based on your race but find it difficult to place you when you are more than one race. They make you feel like you have to choose a race to "behave like." But no one actually thinks of the ugly truth behind what they're saying.

What are you really saying when you say, "You talk like you're white," or "You don't look Puerto Rican"? Stereotypes are the root of racism. Once someone knows your race, they label you or feel like they have it all figured out. In their head, they figured out how you should act. If you do not act like that, you are immediately portrayed as trying to be something you are not.

A lot of racism comes from colorism. You could have two individuals from the same race who will shun the other because of the pigmentation of their skin. A lighter-skinned Hispanic believes they are better than a darker-skinned Hispanic. They believe being darker or having "Black" features makes you less Hispanic. The same applies if you are White or Black. Darker skin is always portrayed as taboo, the same as big hair.

The earlier conversation with Fran about manners is all too familiar. Newark, New Jersey, is my hometown. I have had many encounters in which I was expected to have little to no manners. Thinking back, my most memorable incident made me question why individuals expect specific behaviors. I was with a friend of mine getting ready to start the evening. We were not planning on attending anything formal, so I dressed down in a regular t-shirt, jeans, sneakers and wore my hair in box braids. As we prepared to leave, my friend asked if I'd be willing to meet his other friends. When introduced, I greeted them with a smile, hand outstretched to introduce myself. Instead of being greeted back, I was quickly judged, and the introduction became awkward as the person said, "Aren't you Puerto Rican?"

I then replied, "Yes, and Black."

"Why we shaking hands like this a business transaction or you White or something?"

"That's just how I introduce myself when I meet someone new," I replied. That situation made me rethink the way I introduced myself. I didn't want to be thought of as something I wasn't. Yet, I also did not want to introduce myself the way people thought I should because of my race. It was frustrating to realize that Hispanic and Black individuals were thought of as not having any manners. We were thought of as not being able to be professional, which upset me in so many ways. I went home many days wondering when and why our people started feeling like our race had a certain look, way of speech, and a way of living.

Being biracial or having a biracial child is not easy. You are constantly defending yourself from others. They want you to explain yourself rather than try to understand you. They start to make you feel like you have to justify your actions if you aren't acting according to their idea of who you're supposed to be.

This is where the parents of a biracial child come in. Constant reinforcement is needed because without it; a child is totally clueless as to who they are. There will be times they question who they are, and if the right people provide them with adequate reinforcement, they will not feel like they need to act "how they're supposed to" according to their race.

What does reinforcement look like, you ask? It's reminding a child that they are beautiful just the way they are. They don't need to change and look like more of what others say they should look like. Need I remind you again of what that looks like? Perm, hair falling out, shame. Do not let them experience these same incidents where they question who they are and feel like they have to behave a certain way or look a certain way for acceptance. No, they won't understand at first, but they will thank you for it later.

Reinforcement is the root of a child accepting that they are biracial. They will need to hear reasons why their hair looks different from others, why their complexion is different or why they are shaped this way and that way. These are only examples. It is not easy to cope with being told you are biracial. Over the years, I've come to understand five ways to help a child in their learning process.

One is **Reinforcement**. Sitting down to speak with another biracial woman made me realize something extremely important and relatable even today. Both of us heard many remarks that made us question who we were. In the United States, we regularly encounter individuals who, for some odd reason, believe they know who you are and what you are like solely based on your race. What is more ridiculous is when individuals guess your race or assume your race based on your skin tone or physical features. An example may be, "Hmm, your hair is long, so you must be Hispanic" or "You have a darker tone, so you must be Black." When you do not fit into a stereotype, people start to wonder, and their curiosity can come off as pretty disrespectful.

Research is crucial, which is why I am bringing it up again. Without doing research, you won't know how to console your biracial loved one. Research was my best friend when trying to understand myself. It took a while to understand where I came from. It is much more difficult when you are biracial trying to figure out history from both parents. In some instances, you will not know your child's history and think it isn't important. For biracial kids, it is extremely important because they are trying to find their place. This is when you, as the parent, come in. First, always let a child know that they don't need to behave a certain way! They should behave and talk however they feel most comfortable. As for knowing who they are, do the research with them or on your own and share the information with them.

In today's times, the internet always wins. Most kids spend time on different platforms. Google can help them understand a little bit about their history. There are also books on a lot of topics that can be useful. For example, let's say the child's parent is from Puerto Rico or Jamaica. Your history research can begin with the Taino Indians who inhabited those islands before Christopher Columbus invaded them. This is what helped me understand myself more. Knowing the people I came from and seeing what we've become is empowering.

Listening will be your best friend. In order to fully understand how to help your loved one, effective listening is a must. What you don't want is to make your biracial child feel like their problems don't matter. If they feel like they aren't being listened to, then they'll begin to talk to anyone who will listen. You don't want this! If they talk to the wrong people, those people will feed off of the child's insecurities and tell them things that really aren't good for them. For example, "Oh, just cut your hair, perm it or buy these clothes so you fit in."

Effective listening is important because being biracial is difficult, especially when you don't have someone to relate to. Once a child feels like no one understands them or can relate to them, they start searching for acceptance in the wrong ways. Listen to how they feel and ask them why they feel that way. Often people tell biracial kids what they look like and that they should act accordingly. But as a parent, you need to be the first ear so you can help avoid any peer pressure or prevent any mistakes they'll make trying to fit in.

Hair love is probably the most important for a biracial child. A lot of the time, hair is the way people classify who you are. Is it okay? No! But unfortunately, as a parent, you won't be there for every rude comment someone makes to your child. This is why educating your child on hair love is critical in helping them understand who they are. This may not be necessary if your child has straight hair because straight hair is considered beautiful and acceptable in America. When your hair is curly, puffy, or you deal with shrinkage, the amount of criticism is overwhelming. This is what you'll hear: "Perm it, straighten it, put weave in it, brush it, comb it," and so much more.

Constantly tell your biracial child to forget what people are saying and show them what works for them. Something I had to learn was curly, thick hair is amazing! You don't need a weave, straighteners, or any of that stuff for your hair to be beautiful. There are products that will allow your biracial hair to be healthy and easy to style. Yes, it will take longer, but that's okay because who said beauty was easy to maintain? No one!

Hair love will be tough for your biracial child because they just want to blend in. But you know what you can say? **The best people never blended in. They always stood out!** Barack Obama stood out; Meghan Markle stood out; Tia and Tamera Mowry, Zendaya, Swizz Beatz, Cardi B, Nicki Minaj and Carmelo Anthony are all biracial and amazing. Don't let ignorance and stupidity make you feel like beauty has one face because it has many. Who cares what ethnicity you are, who cares what language you can or cannot speak, *who cares if your hair is big! Is your heart big? That's what really matters!*

AFTERWORD

Christina,

This has always been a sensitive subject for me. Talking about you has always been a difficult topic. I finally broke down around 2017 while talking to my best friend. It haunted me that being biracial caused you pain, and I wasn't there to tell you how beautiful you were and how being biracial didn't define you as a person.

This is for my beautiful sister, whom I've never really gotten to know completely. Same father. Different mothers. There's so much I thought we'd face together, but part of me is relieved that you did not have to suffer the way I did. Not having my dad around was painful, and part of me was selfish because I thought we'd be able to battle that loss together.

I tried so many times to reach out, and this is 100 percent true. Although you were younger, I felt like I needed you so that I could feel whole. I had a duty because I was your only older sibling, and never did I want you to feel alone or abandoned.

I remember when we first met. You were six, and I was fifteen. Before our father could introduce us, you yelled in excitement, "It's Arrriiieeelll!" You recognizing who I was felt so overwhelming. Made me feel like the most important person in the world. From that day forward, I knew it was my duty to protect and love you with everything I had in me.

My favorite memory of us is when we were in our father's backyard. It was summer; you were running around yelling. You were excited to teach us Arabic. "'Ana ahibuk' means I love you." Your eyes were big, beautiful, and full of curiosity. You wore your hair in braids because you told your mom you wanted your hair to look like mine.

Bugs flew around everywhere, and I was panicking. Finally, after screaming my head off, our father called you over and said, "Your sister is scared of the bugs." You stormed over and stomped every bug you could see. Afterward, you looked me in my eyes, smiling and saying, "There sis, they'll never bother you again!" From that day, I felt a bond form into something rock solid. You had my back, and I had yours. Never did I imagine growing up without you, but I was forced to. It killed me that I couldn't watch you grow into the woman you are today. It also killed me that I was forced to grow up without you. At only fifteen with no authority, what could I really do?

Discovering years later that you battled being biracial broke me. I locked myself in the room and cried for hours because I felt like a failure as a big sister. I should've been there to battle that with you, help you, and tell you I encountered the same confusion and anger. Not having our dad around was a big downfall for us because we needed him to understand who we were. He was a significant piece, and I hate that we couldn't learn about our heritage through him.

I never told you how I felt because I didn't know how you felt about me. I didn't know what anyone told you about me. I had so many people against me, and I figured they put you against me too. I didn't grow up the way you did, so a part of me felt as if I was beneath your standards, and I had nothing to offer as an older sibling. Part of me even felt like you were better off without me because I did not grow up wealthy. Although it was not my fault or my family's, I always felt ashamed to be ripped away from you because I could have been there for all the things money couldn't buy. Although I couldn't provide wealth, I could and still can provide unconditional love.

When we did get together, we didn't know how to be around each other. I never completely knew what type of person you were and didn't want to scare you off. But I desperately wanted to know you and wanted a sister relationship.

Now it's 2020 as I'm writing this, and I feel like, wow, what do I do now? I want to bond for so many reasons, but mainly because I'm used to my role as the oldest sibling because my mom has three who are younger than I am. The pain of knowing I'm not guiding you is excruciating. My biggest fear is of you getting older and feeling alone, not understanding that I'll always be here for you no matter how long it takes. I'm waiting with open arms. I AM MY SISTER'S KEEPER.

YOU HAVE 1ST 2ND AND 3RD GENERATIONS OF LATINOS THAT MAYBE DOESN'T SPEAK THE LANGUAGE BUT THAT DOESN'T MAKE THEM ANY LESS PROUD OF THE CULTURA

~ ADRIENNE BAILON-HOUGHTON